NATURAL
STATE

D1519705

JON TRIBBLE

GLASS LYRE PRESS

Copyright © 2016 Jon Tribble
Paperback ISBN: 978-1-941783-15-3

All rights reserved: except for the purpose of quoting brief passages for review, no part
of this book may be reproduced or transmitted in any form or by any means, electronic
or mechanical, including photocopying, recording, or by any information storage and
retrieval system, without permission in writing from the publisher.

Cover art: David Tribble
Design & layout: Steven Asmussen
Copyediting: Linda E. Kim
Author photo: Allison Joseph

Glass Lyre Press, LLC
P.O. Box 2693
Glenview, IL 60026

www.GlassLyrePress.com

for my family, especially my mother and father, and for Allison

To Mike & Mary,

May all your words

come naturally!

In friendship,

[signature]

3/14/16

CONTENTS

I

II

III

Acknowledgments
About the Author

"… I longed to know the world's name."
   —Robert Penn Warren, "American Portrait: Old Style"
   Now and Then: Poems, 1976–1978

THE GARDEN

On summer days there was no escape
from the heat and horseflies growing
out of the rich red clay. Twilight,

Grandfather took the green water hose
to the middle of his truck garden.
You have to wait. Water boils on eggplants'

leaves, puckers tomatoes like yellow raisins.
If he caught me pulling young carrots,
he arced a rainbow of water over me,

leaving behind a trail in the dry rows
like chicken tracks after a morning shower.
A ragged mockingbird dangled

from a live oak's branch, strung there
with a foot of barbed wire just out of dogs'
and grandchildren's reach. *Best scarecrow*

in the world, Grandfather would laugh,
and he planted sweet corn beneath the dead bird.
Rabbits crept from the cotton dawn and dusk

so he kept a shotgun, box of 12-gauge shells,
handy, but I never saw him use it.
Some evenings we sat on the back steps

shelling black-eyed peas. If he saw a rabbit,
he yelled and clapped, stomped his foot
against the wooden steps, might even

get up and throw a rock, but when
we finished he had me carry the paper bag
full of pods to spread at the cotton's edge.

Other nights, when summer storms
scared lightning from the heat-heavy sky,
we sat in the parlor—his whiskey out of sight,

the dogs wrestling underneath the house,
yips and growls slipping up through
the pine floorboards. I curled against

his blue overstuffed chair as he quietly
spit into a coffee tin he kept nearby.
Once, we watched Gila monsters crawl across

his little black-and-white portable.
It was a *National Geographic Special*
and the storm echoed in white flashes of static

with each strobe of lightning. He was washing
butterbeans in a big red bowl of cold water,
and every few minutes he would cough hard

and spit, catch me peeking up at him, and smile.
One spring, two starlings nested
in the chimney of the bedroom where

all of his eleven children had been born.
Grandfather blocked the flue tightly
with a bundle of rags, then went and got

a ladder out, climbed up on the roof
and dropped a smoke bomb down.
When the starlings didn't appear,

he covered the top of the chimney
with plywood, and I ran, couldn't stand
the cries of the birds—even through brick—

had to outrun his echoing laughter.
Beneath the mockingbird's shadow,
the garden was freshly furrowed, manure

dark in new trenches. The cotton fields
were still only rows of red clay,
and in the distance I saw dogs chasing crows

off the road. I heard Grandfather calling me,
and I turned back toward the house
to help clear the rooms of smoke.

CACTUS VIC AND HIS MARVELOUS MAGICAL ELEPHANT

To take revenge on an enemy, buy him an elephant.

—Nepali adage

When Cactus Vic cruised up in his Wonder Bread truck,
it wasn't show business—not quite—but it was the closest thing to it
when I was six, seven, and eight. All the best birthday parties hired him
to arrive as we grew tired of pin-the-tail and kissing games,
the helium balloons no longer fascinating and floating away.
Wonder Bread furnished him with a merry-go-round for three,
sticky fruit pies and Ding Dongs he pulled magically from behind our ears—

I doubt we'd have sat still without them. No rabbits or doves in his show,
instead he poured milk into rolled-up newspaper, waved yellowing white
handkerchiefs with a clown's flourish and grace, and he kept on reminding us
of "the importance of nutrition for a growing body" like a cafeteria worker
shilling Thursday's mystery meat. When I was eight, he'd already become
a depressing sideshow at parties you had to go to because your mother
was somebody's friend or she wanted into this club or that circle.

Wonder Bread retired him, took back the truck, merry-go-round,
and nutrition, and they almost got his name until he called a lawyer.
To make up for all he didn't have while he fought the bakery,
he started giving away plastic animals and miniature New Testaments.
As a gesture of goodwill to make the bad news go away, Wonder Bread
staged a retirement ceremony to award him a parting gift—a baby elephant,
Thaddeus. He emblazoned Cactus Vic & His Marvelous Magical Elephant

on the side of a horse trailer, and the first time he drove up to a birthday party
pulling it behind his new red van, he had our full attention.
It started out the same old stuff, though he seemed puzzled, out of sync,
kept repeating a tired needle through the balloon trick until it popped,
and he stared blankly at us, asked, "Why are we here?"
But then he opened the trailer, led Thaddeus out, and introduced us.
We circled the elephant, petting it shyly, tentative strokes barely making

contact with the strange skin, while Cactus Vic brought out cans of paint.
He pried the tops off, rolled back his sleeves and, with one hand dripping yellow
and the other trickling purple, invited us to join him. We rushed forward,
scooping and splattering handfuls of paint to slap and spread on the gray skin,
coating ourselves and Thaddeus until we were no longer children and elephant,
but orange and pink and green pygmies, rejoicing in screams and laughter
as we danced around our idol in living tribute like the Blue Men of Britain

celebrating fertility, like the Israelites in the Wilderness before the Golden Calf
while they were still unshackled from the tablets and the covenants to come.
Our tender hands caressed the hide, intertwined with other fingers
in our common supplication as the brush of trunk welcomed us closer,
steadied us together. When somebody's mother wandered out from iced tea
and highballs, Cactus Vic didn't work many more parties.
He faded into selling handpainted posters around town, and someone told me

he managed to get his son a job at Wonder Bread after the boy got back
from the Marines, though I heard it didn't work out. But more and more
I find myself wondering about Thaddeus. I hope he's somewhere better
than a zoo, uncaged, in a place he might find himself again in a circle
of worshipers caressing his heavy skin like Indian elephant handlers touch
their mounts to honor Ganesh, a god who reincarnated himself as an elephant,
willing to serve as a beast of burden and be praised for his quiet animal strength.

First Rites: Devil's Den State Park

My father lifted fire
from the shallow yellow light
of September's setting sun,
cupped it in his hands
as if to pour it on us

and we watched wide-eyed,
mostly boys of eleven, twelve,
thirteen on our first campout,
all new scouts, tenderfoots
huddled together by new tents.

Not knowing the difference
between ritual and religion,
we braced against the wind
washing out of the hollows,
mumbled fake Quapaw names

as my father—who was no longer
my father, but a chief who
could swallow the sun—renamed
us Otter and Little Wing,
as he stirred the embers

until the sparks wrapped his head
in a war bonnet of red stars.
He passed the canteen and we drank
the bitter, dark juice he'd saved
from Communion the previous

Sunday. There was no host
to accompany it, but somehow
we knew our bodies replaced
the bread, and in the caves and hills
we tumbled through all weekend

we left plenty of skin and blood
behind to mark this passage,
staining the territory our own
until the valley's winds
could blast it clean again.

Tunnel

Jamie and Chigger were small enough
    to ride their bikes without taking off
        their heads, but the rest of us pushed

ours through the humming darkness,
    green fluorescent water spilling out our end
        on those summer days we gathered

to cross under to Jelly's Auto Salvage.
    Semis above the earthquakes we feared—
        and halfway through pulled in the walls—

the heavy greedy dirt shivering above us.
    Jelly's oily fat hands wrapped ours when
        he let us reach across, pull the levers

on the crusher, compress the old junkers
    into jigsaw boxes. He offered his wide lap
        in the crane where he drew up rusted

Chevys and Fords in the magnet's palm,
    and we dreamed of being lifted as high,
        but we didn't trust he'd release us

before the squeeze. No one believed Jamie's
    tale, how he found the Rolls ornament—
        silver-winged lady—and Tree and Bobby

dragged him kicking into the tunnel's maw,
        pushed him down and left him on his knees
                beside his broken trophy. *Jelly's sweetheart*

hissed back to us while we took our turns
        and I closed my eyes like I was squinting,
                skittered my rock toward the sobbing darkness.

FATHERS

His hands touch mine
like a fly landing
on my fingers. I don't know
if he touches me so softly
because he thinks I will break
or he will break. If I move
my hand to hold his
he is gone, and acts as if
he'd never been there.
I saw him with his father—
before the old man withered
from whiskey and cigarettes—
talking about the North Alabama sun
when the old man suddenly
wrapped his arms around him.
My father's face twisted
to be touched so closely
with no chance of escape.
His arms stayed frozen
at his sides as if the hug
had crushed them,
and he stood answering his father,
hands almost reaching up,
but unable to pull away from his legs.
I'd never try to hug him
after that, or even touch his hand
unless to test him, and I know
he'd never fail, nor I succeed.

Conversations with the Dead

My father's conversation with the dead
today begins as he is sweeping up
the petals which are littering the floor
at the funeral home where he now works.

This new career he has retired into
as greeter, chauffeur, counselor of grief
attires him every day in the crisp suits
and stiff-collared shirts that characterize

the male clientele displayed in quiet rooms
of mourning and remembrance, though
his application of cologne sometimes exceeds
all but the dead can bear. He likes to talk

to the attending families, the friends and co-workers
who gather or wander in between decisions
on flowers and pillows and coffin, verses or eulogies
or music that will sound the resonance of memory

which orchestrates each distinct service of passing
over or on or away or out from lives
whose shifting foundations resist the final note
these souls have tuned and played.

The conversations and details paint the sets
of the stories my father likes to share at dinner
or on weekends in the yard when he recounts
the young man in the extra-long box who was laid out

in tennis shoes and T-shirt, or the lady whose toy
schnauzer accompanied her beneath the ground—
the dog freeze-dried to nestle in the embalmed arms.
He learns of jobs and children, hobbies and possessions

—some too dear to leave behind—and all of this
keeps him coming back, pulls him away
from the mornings and afternoons of CNN
and talk radio which have trained him to speak

to what's not there, so much so that it is impossible
not to picture him singing softly the hymns
his mental jukebox cycles, jingles and television
themes that repetition's barbs have hooked him with,

humming and serenading the still company
he keeps in the draped parlor. But it is not only music,
and he must mutter random thoughts, mumble
questions and feign the answers unspoken

by still voices the way he argues with Rush or
Paul Harvey or nods before agreeing with Larry King.
He will not go silent himself with so many things
left to say and away from the living

in marble halls a short step from the tomb,
he has found the ideal audience who always listens,
never tires, and whose response is exactly what he hopes
it will be each time they find time to chat.

Play Pretties

Castoff jewelry box of cardboard
and velvet my mother filled with
a seven-toothed whalebone comb,

five red-green-yellow-blue-white
aggies, three Mercury dimes, a lava
rock her oldest brother said washed

up on the shore in Honolulu, two
broken dollhouse curio mirrors
from a rummage sale, a polished brass

whistle on a blue cord, a silver
ribbon from Christmas, a pink ribbon
from her sixth birthday, a black

and gold ring with an anchor inset
on the ebony stone, a small photo
of Clark Gable clipped from a local

paper, a bigger photo of Shirley Temple
from *Life,* a rabbit's foot, a chipped
cameo, two shriveled buckeyes, and

a yellowing photo of her father posing
with a walking cane on a sunny afternoon
before she could remember losing him.

Imago Mundi

We left our familiar country
for Tuscumbia's humid haze—
the summer's heavy breath
exhaled at dawn and dusk—

those yellowing halls of tiny
flaking roses, wallpaper stained
with dust and reminders of
the shabby roof and cracked eaves.

The children of her children,
we returned each year to disappear
into the peach crates and Sears &
Roebuck boxes, looting the past

while parents sipped iced tea
on the veranda, slick rings
sweating on the weathered white
paint from Mason jars now make-

shift glasses. Grandmother's
voice slipped between the cicadas
and mockingbirds those hazy
evenings, but we children were

lost to that quiet music. We
wrapped ourselves in gold-
paged volumes of Bulfinch,
brilliant plates of Perseus

dripping adders from the Gorgon's
head, Valhalla and its rainbow
bridge, the shadowed Cupid
standing over Psyche's bed.

We knew the faded smiles
of Gable and Dietrich, Munich's
goosestep echoes from graying
photos in *Life* magazine.

We could trace the maps of
Ptolemy and Mercator on heavy
rolled-up facsimiles, pace
a world flat or round where

Leviathan lifted itself spouting
from the waves; the Winds with
names like flowers and faces
like the out-of-work men who

gathered on the corners waiting
for field work picking cotton,
yard work trimming privet hedge.
We burrowed in those papers and

books looking for something
missing from the family photos,
grade school, high school, college
diplomas hanging throughout

the house. In that back hall
we were hidden from adult eyes,
our only chaperones three women
on an aging oriental tapestry…

twilight closes like a curtain
as she reaches for the rose-pale
blossoms, garlands her sisters
entwine to wreath the coal-black

buns hiding cascades of hair
they braid for one another
each night. Now, green parrots
preen, stretch in these last rays

of warmth; nearby, the ibis
stands as sentinel guarding
the laughter; a breeze sways
the living canopy while

the youngest girl haltingly
strums a mandolin, forgetting
and remembering the next line
of her sisters' favorite ballad.

The eldest twirls her parasol
till golden carp swimming on its
blue field blur into sunbursts
of flame—comet-fish all head

and tail and burning light.
The red and black ceramic
planters, bonsai enameled on
the slick surfaces; smooth stones

cradling the artificial pond's
mirror-image of the sisters;
the skeleton of architecture
peeking through silver leaves

and branches—a column here,
a wooden railing, the ghost
of an arch; the pink kimono's
petals splashing from the silk,

the red's mountains rising over
well-concealed legs, the jade
green dragon wrapping furiously
over the youngest sister's back;

all of these things belie
the pleasant occidental faces
staring out from the garden,
illusion of another world...

We are almost there ourselves,
but here public fountains stand
dry beneath statues of Rebel
heroes, empty buses roll brusquely

through the sweltering streets.
Corner dancers in Muscle Shoals
have stored away their bottle-
cap taps, "Dixie," and buck &

wing. Recklessly, dragonflies
buzz through thick afternoons
and we ignore the whispers
from the porch—Selma, Birmingham,

Montgomery, Memphis, Little Rock.
Tuscumbia is quiet; safe.
Town bells here ring out only
for Sunday service, funerals.

Pursuit of Happiness

When Jayson Williams of the NBA's New Jersey Nets
repeats for the third time, *A man can pay another man*

whatever he wants—it's in the Constitution, you point
me to the bookshelf where I finally find the document,

We the People, Articles, Amendments, and all the rest
in *The Universal Almanac 1996,* and we argue if equal

protection or emancipation or interstate trade can stretch
like Silly Putty and pull capitalism from these words

like color images of Dick Tracy I leached onto the flesh-
colored pancake I rolled and unrolled from its plastic

egg in Little Rock twenty years before this reference's
namesake year. We survived the return of "Philadelphia

Freedom" that summer of '76, but the fall was "(Don't
Fear) the Reaper" and ninth-grade Civics where *Our*

Republic taught the difference between democracy's vox
populi and the John Birchers at the State Fair whose

flag declared on the white stripes, *America Is A Republic*
Not A Democracy! Thank The Lord For The Difference!

When my mother found out Chip's Barbeque's owner
was their leader, she stopped going despite her craving

for the corn dogs and the best lemon meringue pie—
we all make sacrifices for our freedom. Though Edward

Hicks's *The Peaceable Kingdom* wanly smiled down from
our mantel those days at 2000 Aldersgate Road, my

mother's savior from three adolescents and her mother's
cancer came over the counter in blue ovals of Cope,

which helped soften the hours between calls like light
slipping beneath an opal's surface, warm and cool

iridescence coalescing. I can't refract such memories
the way I might bend a story of someone I'll never meet,

but I think I learned enough to know no one pays
anyone enough for what is given, we all pay too much

for what is free, and no declaration of independence
provides liberty and inalienable rights like we think it does.

Lunar Eclipse

Stretched back in a lawn chair,
       I sat beside my mother rocking
in our gravel driveway, and tried
       to follow the line her finger
drew to the stars, but the sky
       was too clear, the points
too numerous. Where did the Crab
       scuttle away from the Hunter's

club? What hid the seven faint
       stars she called the Maidens?
They were fleeing from lovers
       who chased them into the heavens,
and she said when she worked
       with her sisters picking cotton
each September break Alabama schools
       gave for families to bring in

the crop, her sister Helen told
       the story of the Maidens and
their flight from love that left
       them as dim stars on the horizon.
The story helped keep them going
       as dusk came on and the bolls
left the girls' hands bloody, so
       sore even the hour-long soak

in Epsom salts her mother made all
        the girls do didn't really help.
They pulled burrs from each others'
        hair, brushed out the buns they
wore in the fields with the comb
        of whalebone a great-grandmother
had left in the family, then
        the six of them took turns by age

at the mirror and basin, put on
        their flannel gowns, and took
their places in the room's two
        featherbeds. She asked me what
they had taught us in school about
        eclipses and I told her of Norse
myths, wolves swallowing the sun
        and moon—something I had read

in Bulfinch—but she said she thought
        it resembled nothing so violent.
I woke as the last white sliver
        vanished. She was humming a song
I didn't recognize, improvising
        her melody around the poor man's
widow's calls from back among
        the pines. She leaned up, touched

my arm, said I should go to bed,
> but I asked her to let me stay
until the moon reappeared. So
> we sat in silence as a point
grew at the edge of the black
> disk that had replaced the moon,
but the light wasn't what I'd hoped
> for, only slight and yellow.

Up and Down Wye Mountain

Daffodils crowning the summit
of this country church-topped hill
   have begun to pale and wither

from the sun and heat of Arkansas
   summer, though the earlier
hymn of the flowers' open mouths

   brought out the city dwellers
to the festival the congregation
   here celebrates every year.

But it is the church itself which
   calls us, our pilgrimage
a journey to familiarize my mother

   with this site and one other
the Bishop appointed her to lead.
   Her recent vocation has been

rehearsed with sermons, ceremonies,
   and assisting in the rituals
that embody the articles of faith,

   reaching beyond response
which a lifetime of supplication
   has taught to lead the call,

but, at sixty-eight, she now seeks
     to test the strength of her
calling anew, to discover if this

     challenge is the path study
and long prayer mean to bring her to.
     My father, my wife, and I

have joined today, all of us, perhaps,
     a bit skeptical and concerned,
but also warmed by the enthusiasm

     apparent in my mother's
sharp attention to all the practical
     concerns: how long it takes

to drive from home, gas stations
     or their lack upon the way,
the safe and unsafe speeds to wend

     this single winding trail.
My wife steps out first and then
     the rest of us stretch

and gaze about at this calming
     scene, the handiwork
of masons resting under the oaks.

The stone church appears
to be locked tight, but a back door
  guarded only by a blue-

bellied lizard opens and we enter.
  There is much more here
than any of us had dared hope for:

  kitchen, Sunday school
meeting room, an organ and piano,
  and the simple solid altar

and cushioned pews the sanctuary
  presents us with exceed
every expectation and demonstrate

  the care of belief and duty
we might or might not find evident
  in storied sacristies

housing relics of less humble
  design. Attendance
figures from the Sunday before

  show "38" adults on hand,
"15" children, and a collection
  of "$143.85" with "$20"

added for building and grounds.
   My father wants a picture,
and though my mother refuses to

   pose for him, my wife
and I take turns standing behind
   the sturdy Communion rail.

We head down the hill to Bigelow,
   six miles away by road
—though the hawks we see rising

   in the bright sky might
make the distance less than three—
   and my mother wonders aloud

why two small congregations are not
   one, though she says she
would not rush either church toward

   a change neither might want.
As we reach the bottom of Wye Mountain,
   the rich flood plain for

the Arkansas River slopes through
   stands of pine and tangles
of honeysuckle on to Toadsuck Ferry

where the now lock-and-dam
tamed waters are traversed much more
easily, though perhaps less

often since busy interstates have
cut off these back roads.
Bigelow approaches with promise

at first, a horse farm
shadowed back amidst the loblolly,
a cattle ranch with heavy

Bhraman hybrids sinking in a stock
pond's cool mud. But as
we near the single railroad track

which marks this town as
here—along with its beige aluminum-
sided post office—houses

begin to seem to sway as much from
poor construction and
disrepair as from the humid heat.

Our first attempt to find
the church finds us turning around
at the mobile home assembly

yard that must be this town's only
    industry, though scattered
insulation and a cemetery of unused

    metal frames appear to be
permanent monuments to prosperity
    long past. A second try

leads us back and forth dead-end
    one-way streets, but there
are few enough that by process

    of elimination we end up
in front of what a weathered sign
    tells us is the "United

Methodist Church," though easily
    we could have mistaken
the style of the scrawl painted

    here for a "For Sale By
Owner" posting. With no apparent
    parking site and the ditches

flanking the road choking with tall
    weeds, I ease the car
onto the crossover leading up to

the white wooden building
which teeters on its cinderblock
    foundation. The squat

steeple points toward heaven only
    indirectly, seemingly
concerned in this world with

    the thin shade in sight
some hundred yards away. My wife
    and father get out, but

I remain with my mother, who now
    gasps a bit from the close
air. She fans herself and tells

    how this church has lost
members to death and relocation
    the last decade, how fewer

than two dozen names appear on
    the current roll—maybe
fifteen or twelve active members:

    not a growing ministry.
The job here would be staying
    the decline and, perhaps,

attracting a new congregation,
      though from where is—
at best—unclear. When my wife

   and father return with
the word that the building is
      locked, their survey

of the exterior is grim indeed:
      rotting doors stacked
carelessly against the outside

   of the church, mildew
and what unstained paint there is
      flaking and peeling off

—an erratic layer of dandruff
      spotting the surrounding
ground—, no visible electric lines,

   —though a rusted-out
window unit belied the absence
      of power—, and stairs,

front and back, warped and loose
      and waiting for any
misstep to send someone tumbling.

"Someone should burn
it to the ground," my father says,
   despite forty-five years

working for and with the Methodist
   Church. "If you've got
a match, I'll do it right now."

   But my mother is calm.
She says this challenge is what
   she prayed for. We all

wonder how this forgotten church
   has kept its charter,
but slowly my mother's resolve

   takes hold of us doubters
until my father even begins saying
   he will transfer membership

to this church, work with them
   to clean and shore up
the damage. We drive back past

   the chapel atop the hill
on our way home, understanding
   a little more the devotion,

the need to serve which shapes
   my mother's calling.
A week later, the Bishop joins

   my parents for their
introduction to the congregation
   of ten at Bigelow and

the members of the church welcome
   my mother and father.
Then the Bishop tells the church

   how happy he is to find
them supportive of this newly
   licensed minister on her

first appointment, and suddenly
   the recognition strikes
them, they want to know what

   the Bishop thinks he is
trying to pull on them, that surely
   he doesn't expect them

to receive sacraments from a woman.
   Recounting this later,
my mother says, "It was as if I

were no longer there
the moment they realized I was,"
   and her voice is weary,

even as she goes on to describe
   her surprise at the beauty
of the sanctuary: six tapestries

   resplendent on the walls
following the Gospel of Christ's
   nativity, His ministry,

the Last Supper, Gethsemane,
   the Trial before Pilate,
and Calvary's hill. New hymnals

   rested beside dog-eared
Bibles in the plush red-velveted
   pews. She said they had

polished the brass to impress their
   new pastor, decorating
the heavy oak altar with yellow lilies

   bowing beneath the dark
shining wood of the empty cross
   suspended from the rafters.

MAGNOLIA

Bending back rigid branches, we disappear in the cave of green,
carpet of brittle question-mark leaves crackling with each step
we take toward the thick trunk. We hide together. Squeals and
calls echo around us as brothers and sisters, neighborhood friends

uncover "best" hiding places under bridges, beneath pine needles,
in bone-dry creek beds, secreted among squirrels' nests in a slippery
elm. We back against gray bark, slick and muscled like skin,
gather leaves, the spiny remains left by blossoms gone to seed,

quilt fallen limbs over our own arms and legs. Wrapped close
in this blanket, we poke and prod each other with the hard fruit
of the magnolia, daring our laughter, our small pains and discomfort
to reveal us. The heavy sweet decay of last month's white blossoms

fills every breath sneaking past our tight lips. We shiver off
centipedes and grubs twitching on shins and calves, tickling
the backs of thighs, traversing the smooth landscape of our bodies.
In these shadows we almost become one heartbeat, one whisper of lungs.

But we do not touch; we do not join; we do not turn and embrace
anything other than concealment. The magnolia is our cloak and
nothing more. We will slip away from its shadows and come out
when we hear the yell, "All's free," and we will forget about that tree.

THE DAY AFTER ELVIS DIED

Bused home from two-a-days,
junior high players in half-shirts
and padless football pants howling
like hound dogs, swaying back
and forth in the aisle with a tick

of horny release stuttering from
hips snaking in slow circles, one
leg posted down while the other
spasmed with grand mal energy,
she kept staring at us in her wide

security mirror, tugging and chewing
back anger and a loose strand
of her off-yellow hair, and when
she swung us sharply toward
an off-ramp of the Wilbur Mills

Freeway—an unscheduled turn
in our course toward home—lurched
to an air-braked shudder and stop
on the right shoulder, she stood,
said we could all go straight to hell,

and walked off leaving the door
almost as wide open as our eyes
and hangdog mouths. The keys
dangled in the ignition, but none
of us dared start the bus, and a few

guys grabbed their cleats, trudged
down the steps, but the rest of us
were too salt-drained, tired, and
sure she had to come back, couldn't
abandon us and this job in such

a gesture of misplaced loyalty.
Half an hour later, someone said
she lived nearby, so with keys
in hand we trooped over to her little
blue house behind War Memorial

Golf Course. Two of the older boys
approached the door while most
of us settled in the dusty yard or
milled about stretching sore legs
or hoisting duffel bags in mock

power lifts, grunting as if locked
under the weights back in the gym.
After polite, then firm, then loud
knocking, she answered out a screen
window, saying clearly she'd shoot

any one of us bastards still on her
property in thirty seconds. Like
some frantic free-for-all drill we
scattered, knocking one another
spinning and down and back up

and over the chain-link fence, contact
fiercer than we would ever make
on the playing field that August
where potbellied coaches drained
our fury under the Arkansas sun.

Every Day

after Robert Hayden

Here the muddy river wraps its current
about this shoal, makeshift island planted
with dogwood, plum, and apple blossom.

Here my sister and her son gather petals,
early summer snow of flowers carpeting
red clay and concrete anchoring this place.

Here barges plow the flat dark water,
their wakes tumbling the reflected bridges,
city of empty cotton brokers and bail bonds.

Here a glass pyramid mirrors back the scowl
trembling across my nephew's face as his
garlands spill from his arms and scatter.

Here gulls from down- and upriver spin wild
above shiny gar rolling through schools
of shad, bloated buffalo, and catfish surfacing.

Here my sister cradles her son to her,
reclining on this grassy knoll lifted beyond
courts and chances, promises and denials.

Here the past is last night's dog races, last
year's tornadoes, the Mississippi full of chains,
bones, broken rudders and paddlewheels.

Here before flight she holds her son against
a future neither sees beyond the morning,
afternoon, evening, night of uncertainty.

Here the wind lifts the petals over the city
and the boy sleeps, dreams only of his hands,
his mother, and flowers of the South.

ANAXIMANDER LEWIS

Mr. Jones kicked him out
of the Horace Mann High School Band

when he went solo during the flag line's
routine, blowing notes that left the purple

and gold material hanging limp
from the still poles. It didn't

slow him down. He hitched weekends
to Memphis, catching sets on Beale Street

at any club he could sneak in.
I still played contrabass

clarinet when I met him and wanted music
so bad I practiced till my lips bled,

but it just got me sore lips.
Anaximander tried to help, told me

to love the reed, not fight it,
feel the bass line growing out of my back,

through my arms and fingers,
out the bell of the horn.

I couldn't do it, quit the school band
when he was kicked out—there just wasn't anything

worth hearing anymore. I sold the contrabass
and bought an old car, started driving him

to Memphis on the weekends. He talked
about how his grandfather was the first

Lewis to learn to read,
how he named his children and grandchildren

after philosophers, hoping they'd all
grow up men and women of knowledge. Anaximander

laughed at that, said the only thing he read
was music, once

for each song, after the first time
he felt the notes, knew what should go next

and how long to hold it. He let me paint *Aperion*
on his clarinet case (as close as I could get

to the Greek of his namesake) and he played that horn
like something elemental, like he could

transmute breath as it passed over the reed
into notes that burned out the bell.

Dogwood Creek

Little jesuses on the water,
she says as she kisses the handful
of petals and tosses them
into the slow current.

The crosses hidden in the blossoms
spin and most catch and gather
behind the fallen log
damming the minnow pool.

Later she'll take my hand,
hold it against her breast.
Count my heartbeats, she says,
and tell me what it means.

Whisper Trees

What I can't remember is the color
of her blouse, though I know the way

the sun lit her blond hair as he
brushed it free with his fingers,

the blue barrettes she always wore
joining the growing pile of their

clothes. I was eleven, always
following her to the lake where she

worked summers as a lifeguard, and
when I saw them go into the woods

I trailed behind, stalking them like
an Iroquois brave from the *Leather-*

stocking Tales, avoiding the dry twigs
better than Natty Bumppo ever did.

They stopped within a grove of pine,
loblolly and broadleaf branches green

clouds against the blue sky, and I
watched as he pulled her to him,

lowered her to the brown blanket
of needles. There was little cover

so I stretched belly-down in a ditch
that would have been a creek in spring

or autumn, turned the flat shale rocks
around me to find centipedes, trails

of silver and white lines left by grubs
and earthworms, a stain of calligraphy

that I could no more decipher than
I could understand why she came here.

When I looked up, he was on top of her
and they rocked together so slowly

I had to watch her knees carefully
to catch them slide farther out, her

hands slip lower and lower on his back
to pull him closer in. I was glad

I couldn't see her face. Their bodies
marked by shadows and tan lines, new

white skin unnatural, uncovered despite
the pine branches reaching down to them,

but I kept watching, still, unable
to make anything out of the echoes of

their voices in the trees, unable to
imagine myself ever in his place.

WHITE BOY WITH AFRO

In '75 when P-Funk and Led Zeppelin
separated black and white in Little Rock
as surely as National Guardsmen
had enforced Eisenhower's will
in that inverted year at Central High,
the brushouts grew tall on the heads
of dark and light men and women
whose crowns announced to anyone
looking for close-crop, burrhead,
nappy, or congolene that the sheen was in
and Black Power fists at the end
of plastic picks were political weapons
of style if not consciousness.
Like the hippie locks and flattop
confrontations of the last decade,
these tonsorial battlelines clearly demarked
from fifth grade forward the side of the cafeteria
each belonged to, which locker to
turn around to open, not to mention
the bus rides. And that left me.
A wavy-headed, wire-haired
thirteen-year-old whose scalp
prickled uncomfortably at the thought
of ever again setting foot in the shop
of the fat bald barber who always promised
to make me look just like him.
These dirty little wars offered few allies.
As weeks passed into months between haircuts,

I became more suspect with each
thickened morning. When crewcuts
on the offensive line threatened to pin me down
while the razor made sure that helmet could fit
over the mess, my fastest teammates—
most in the backfields or wideouts—
kidded about touching up my 'fro,
lifting the top to avoid those flattening wings
which looked more like Bozo than Shaft.
And everyone joked about woodpiles.
But it wasn't all jokes, and when I fell behind
crossing back from the Mad Butcher
where we all piled in for Gatorade
or Jungle Juice during two-a-days,
three high schoolers stopped me
at the break in the fence before
I could slip through. One of them,
the slightest of the three since beating down
a seventh-grader wouldn't be much
of an accomplishment, flipped the pick
from its perch on his head like a switchblade
might be flicked out of a back pocket,
and snapped, *Use this, boy.*
I took it and, turning my wrist
so the teeth faced my scalp
like a trowel in my grip would face the earth,
prepared to disentangle the matted, sweaty
mass atop my head, when the biggest reached over

and gently pulled the pick from my grasp
and handed it back to the first,
who glanced at his friends' smiles
and then smiled at me,
slapped me on the back, and said, *You're cool.*

DRIVER'S SCHOOL

> *If I feel physically as if the top of my head*
> *were taken off, I know this is poetry.*
> —Emily Dickinson

He was a screamer, called us
      drunks, punks, low-life scum,
said he'd see we never get
      back on the streets, behind
the wheel if he had any say,

and every Thursday night showed
      the same film, *Red Asphalt,*
baby jammed between rear wheel
      and fender, arms and legs
scattered across the median,

marionettes and dummies almost
      indistinguishably slumping
as if all strings were cut,
      nothing tangible left to hold
anything together. All of it

courtesy of the California Highway
      Patrol, even the title shot
of a windshield suddenly splashed
      with blood, its wipers sweeping
against the red downpour.

The first weeks I saw a billboard
        Jesus in my mind, Mississippi's
own "Bloody 98" snaking through
        Spanish moss and rusting tin
shacks, waiting to "claim

another victim: Will you be next?"
        Shortcut to Mobile, Destin,
Panama City two-week drunks, shot-
        and-beer-nights of easy, teenage,
no-name, sweaty, sloppy groping.

But the shock wore off. Four or
        five weeks in, during the scene
where they use the Jaws of Life,
        cut the driver out of contorted
scrap metal, and the paramedics

try to lift him slow only to have
        the top of his head slip off
like a dime-store hairpiece—
        I couldn't help it, giggling,
then snickering, then full out

laughing. All the sergeant's
        redneck threats and nightstick
waving couldn't stop it. Then
        it spread. The woman who wore
her rabbit coat through every

class, the four Latino guys who
      huddled whispering Spanish,
the young black men and women
      who came in couples, the old
men who always got here first,

claiming the back rows so they
      could sleep, all of us joining
in laughter, people who had
      never spoken to one another
drowning out the tired warnings,

giddy and ashamed, joyously alive.

PERS'NAL USE

I never knew you as Rooster, scratching out
"the king of the barnyard" on an old six-string,
hole worn through the back from thirty years
of rubbing your leg when the second or third
set got hot and long. Only Mr. Lester to me,
selling policies door-to-door or when the whiskey
burned the back of my throat while you laughed
at the smoothness. You taught me losing—

cutting cards for drinks always bought with my
commission—said you were saving up for
a little house in Helena, but you sprung for
tickets when Alberta Hunter played The Peabody
in Memphis. On another deal and cut, I
wound up polishing our shoes, pressing limp
shirts crisp and starch-stiff, while you spent
an hour waxing that ragged little moustache.

You wouldn't let me step on the red carpet,
slipped the waiter a twenty which only got
seats at the side, but you didn't complain,
said we were plenty close, that she had
a striking profile. When this little old woman
crept out, leaned on the mike stand, I knew
you had gone crazy. But she opened her mouth,
and her voice witnessed those long hours

on my feet, hot pavement up and down Elvis
Presley Boulevard when no one's buying,
redstone tenements near St. Jude's where
the hardened unbelievers turn the electric
fan away, make sure none of the breeze
slips out the screen—I looked at your face
and knew the legacy you had handed me.
But then she stopped, changed songs,

and I heard the whisper and cool fingers
of a woman slipping across my weary back
on a Sunday morning that lasts just long enough,
left me wishing I'd grown old as you so she
wouldn't look through me, I'd have a chance
to be her *mechanic,* not blush when she called
for a *long, tall, young one* for her *pers'nal use.*
After the show, you followed me to the edge

of the stage and when she bent down to autograph
my napkin you said, I'm Billy Lester, so quietly
I barely even heard it, but she did and smiled.
She reached out, took both your hands and said,
You look good, Rooster, then asked if you'd
join her for a number, but you shook your head
—she didn't ask again. Walking down Beale
Street you wouldn't say much, only mumbled

about things left behind, but later you gave me
an acetate of a thirty-year-old man and the song
that left him pushing insurance. When your
retirement passed, you moved to Helena, sent
a photo of that white house with sunflowers
towering beside the fence, and I know you'll
write when the river's rising too fast, warn me
to watch out selling what can't be collected.

Amateur Night at the Prime Tyme

Who knew this town had so much flesh in it?
The dancer drops her head between her legs,
and men who can't afford another drink

reach deep to come up with a couple of bucks
to get her to remove another shred of pink
rip-away T-shirt clinging to her shoulders

like junk mail poking from the lip of a mailbox
at an abandoned apartment she left in Malvern
or El Dorado. There is only so much one can pay

to see, but tonight it's here, where leftover
green beer goes for eight bucks a pitcher,
stale popcorn and peanuts two-fifty a basket;

but it's not sustenance they come for unless to feed
a lonely imagination or half-forgotten lust—free
to anyone who's paid the membership fee at the door.

Tomorrow she might be checking out customers
at the Mad Butcher or stocking shelves at 7-Eleven;
she could be calling from Sears or flipping burgers

at Dairy Queen, whatever she wakes for to pay the bills
and rent, invisible behind a smile or frown, cheerful
hello or impersonal grunt. Now she's more spectacle

than any daylight life could shadow, the thong
of her G-string disappearing before the mirror
of blank faces that give back only their reflections,

wives and girlfriends and magazines and passing
glances staring through the gyrations, shimmering from
lubricious skin jiggling along to the forgettable music.

THE BEST CHICKEN IN ARKANSAS

Before those words he started finished,
I knew what wasn't coming from his lips

was this superior fowl of splendid plumage—
Rhode Island Red in my mind, but probably

dead white with a red comb if the feathered
semis streaming across the state are any real

indication of the king of the barnyard—
a bellows-keeled cock-of-the-walk scratching

across Grand Prairie coops where nitrate-
laced sluices shimmy past the slick pools

of nightsoil collecting the last trace of mountain
water the Delta's cotton-poor fields need

to keep beans and rice from choking on
a stewardship of fertilizer and herbicide.

And I knew he wasn't smelling oil and rubber
burning on the ovals underneath the scream

of halogen peeling back the dark as muscle
in primer-coated, cut-angled metal shells

frees the beery crowds from the packed red
earth as demolition reverbs from the thrust

and grip of steel on steel, or the lonelier
knights careening down blank asphalt lanes

until the joust of nerves brakes and shames
back to life the sense all senselessness loathes.

And I knew those words weren't turning for
miniskirts flagging above dark legs in summer's

unforgiving age, merciless musk of locker talk's
bravado, the forty- and fifty-year-old's bane

and brace for the turned head, long backward
glance those men who cross the line transform

into furtive Polaroids of the eighteen-year-old
girlfriend secreted upon them like a flask

to share sparingly, sin to confess only when
illusion shakes loose of mooring and drifts away.

And the adolescent taunt or curse was so far from
these words it was only a splinter of a memory

of a boy we would have named "Chicken Neck"
if he hadn't been "Weasel," his apocryphal

bathroom antics given wing on the jetstream
of teenage opinion, his strangled denials twisted

in whispervine which never cared he never
was invited anywhere by anyone before or after.

No, when those words defined themselves it was
salt and pepper, spices and juice, the crisp sizzle

seizing grease, flour, batter, and bird in a palm
of flavor's sharp rush of sustenance, so I listened

as he told me AQ Chicken was worth five hours
up the Pig Trail from Little Rock to Fayetteville—

if I was ever in Springdale, we would share
the Sunday dinner served every day of the week.

III

From the West

Ex oriente lux

The exhibits wrapped and taped
airtight, glass cases blanketed
against dust, but I still see the jade
stones green as lichen, paper-white

skeletons of prehistoric fish as if
I were five, bolting up the twisting,
tall staircase like shad fear-blinded
swirled back into the gaping toothy

bill of the stuffed alligator gar
suspended above the landing between
flights, its smile a permanent
evolutionary invitation.

This antebellum mansion, the grounds
surrounding it with magnolias like
belles sashaying the air sweet in summer
when luna moths floated from the waxy

leaves like Carnival masks tossed aside
at a reveler's whim—all of this safe,
for now at least, from downtown
developers, landmark status assured

as birthplace to Douglas MacArthur,
though he scarcely claimed the state,
let alone this house in Little Rock.
On my first visit, I wandered until, alone,

I found myself in the aviary, glass-eyed
beaks and tufts taxidermied still,
my stare and clouding breath
the showcase's only sign of life.

I wanted to reach inside, pull the wires
suspending the sparrow hawk
mid-dive, red blue white plumage
a bullet of color in descent.

The crane's yellow legs ridiculously
teetering over me, the pelican's
rubbery throat held me there
until my mother and a guide bustled in.

Today, a group of boys call signals
back and forth across a line of scrimmage,
July touch football on MacArthur Park's
unlined field. It's cooler than Arkansas

July can usually find, but moisture
thickens the slick air. Across the park,
the Art Museum shows off its new statue,
a totem cut from living oak.

The long face and headdress tower
over the front of the squat building,
supports cemented to the Quapaw's
cheeks since the roots have begun to give.

Inside, there are birds, too;
porcelain, arranged with ferns
and a working fountain, and the ouzel
sits so near the splashing water

I'd swear it would get wet.
Full-size reproductions are on sale
in the gift shop, along with turquoise
jewelry. The tribes who once camped

along the Arkansas River left mounds
for their dead and little else.
When the Museum of Natural History reopens,
they will have lighted displays of tools,

arrowheads retrieved from those burial
sites, interactive touch screens
to lead visitors through this past,
a hands-on demonstration

for the archaeologically adventurous.
The football game goes on,
the sides uneven, but enthusiastic.
The scrum has become rougher

as they line up, run and pass,
scramble in a heap at the end of each
play so a touch can't be denied.
If I wanted a glimpse of the river

I'd be out of luck, my only view blocked
by a billboard of the Empire State
Building, the New York City skyline.
The season's right for travel,

but commuters pass back and forth
before that sign each day, speeding
on their way to the North Little Rock Bridge.
The state flag with its segregationist diamond,

a modified Southern Cross, lowers out front,
and I would need to be as high as the flagpole
to see this day end properly, slow barges
drifting out of town, toward the Mississippi.

Hookslide

Down at Ray Winder Field you broke
the monotony of another Travelers'
losing season with an empty popcorn
carton you'd flattened and placed
on the concrete as an imaginary
second base. Fifty feet of baseline
then you hit the floor, ducking
the tag with your body singing out,
arms flailing in misdirection,
ending up huddled on the other side
of the bag. But your foot would hold
and the crowd cheered and bought you
beer all night, your antics replacing
ninth-inning rallies that never came.

In town, you carried a piece of flat
cardboard, plywood, anything that
worked for a target, and you'd set
it down and perform for anyone with
two bucks. Sidewalks, parking lots,
dead-end streets became your runways—
you said you couldn't work on dirt—
and you'd turn your graying Cardinals
cap backwards and throw your sixty-
year-old body into each steal like
the game was on the line every time.
Your retinue of dogs and kids ran
beside you, even tumbled at the end
in a mass of paws and feet and noise.

But the bigtime was at the ballpark,
The Show for you like most of these
bush leaguers shagging lazy grounders
would never know. A standing "O"
when you walked in, the peanut-beer-
hot dog vendors kept the wide aisle
between the stands and box seats clear
for you, hawking from the stairs
to stay out of your way, and someone
let you throw out the ball at games
they couldn't get the Governor, Mayor,
Chief of Police, or anchorperson from
a local station. A groundskeeper
would come up and sweep the aisle clean

then the place became all yours, the chant
HOOKSLIDE HOOKSLIDE HOOKSLIDE
swelling as you bowed deeply to the crowd,
took your stance and eyed the mark you'd set,
small and far away as you began to run.

NIGHTWATCHMAN

It doesn't have to be broken
because I dropped it, my father
yelled on the nights he'd had four
or five or ten and he was on
the roof dropping the spent
Malt Duck bottles off into
the darkness to hear them
crash into shards I'd sweep
later from the bank parking lot.

And I stood in the locked
elevator watching him, the mace
gun full on my belt, black
nightstick softly bruising
my hand with each slap as
he swayed at the edge, ten
stories of air between him
and the broken glass.

It's too cold to be up here,
I'd call across the roof,
but he couldn't or wouldn't
hear me as he launched
the last one toward the street
screaming my name, then fall
back, his hands crossed
over his crotch, head rolling
back and forth on the tar roof.

I'd rest the nightstick
in the elevator and walk
through the wind to gather him
from the edge, supporting him
until we were down and back
on the ground floor. I'd
carry him to the bathroom,
lean him in the nearest stall,
covering his legs with my
jacket, and leave him to
collect at the end of my shift.

SLOW LIGHT

A woman has slowed the speed of light
to thirty-eight miles an hour in the cold
dense substance matter can become,
and they say they'll go slower still, until

a tortoise could race the beam across the room,
and I wonder if we must keep changing
the absolutes like the certainty of tomorrow
or the distance between our life and the door

in and out of it, like when Kenny showed up
after going missing for three days and
in the net his brain gasped within—the week
of yellow jackets and blotter acid—he surfaced

to deliver the best speech of his life
in high school debate, how we all stood
and clapped as he returned to the desk
that might have looked like an open fist to him

or a Ferris-wheel seat that would buck and spin
and lift him closer to the fecal soup, the blood
sluice and steam hoses of the chicken
processing plant in Danville, Arkansas,

the last place I'd heard he landed, how I
would never see again the same eyes in that face
I'd known since first grade, how the finest
moment in our lives may not matter at all.

LABOR DAY

My father's breath conspires against him,
each effort capturing less oxygen as he
struggles with the necessary business of
living. Morphine and age slow his blood
to a stagnant crawl, clots settling hard
in his lungs this September morning.

He asks me to read the news of the morning,
collapse the world to shorthand for him
to grasp, but with each shudder—hard
seconds of pain and doubt no longer he
can ignore—his desperate and blood-
shot eyes clench tight, his last sign of

resistance failing against the constancy of
a body slowing against his will, morning
offering no renewal and healing, blood
carrying no life and sustenance. To him
this goes beyond any understanding he
has reached with his flesh, the hard

realities of age should mean stroke, hard-
ening arteries, paralysis, or the end of
struggle and pain, possibilities which he
accepts as irrevocable, final. But morning
has brought a different problem to him
and he is bewildered by the hesitant blood

within his veins, the obstacle these blood
clots build within his lungs, a tight hard
firewall blocking oxygen burning in him,
the traffic of the body stalled in a morning
pile-up, an accident snarling the passage of
life unconscious within. Helplessly, he

reaches toward me, a weak touch all he
can manage against the betrayal of blood
and breath, and we both know this morning
he must return to the hospital's cold hard
light, the antiseptic flowers an imitation of
life as the blood is thinned within him.

I take his hand, and he tries to force a hard
smile, to acknowledge our deeper bond of blood
this morning which binds him to me, me to him.

We Are Part of the Body

Half-snapped, the thicket of young willows
                leans south, bent like novices learning
      to pray, stiff and self-conscious,
                  pressing their hands together,

a congregation of empty branches. Our
                breath hangs before us like something
      we've forgotten to say, and we kick
                and shake the ice-laden cover

to discover nothing beneath. Dim
                tracks which could be deer, rabbit,
      a five-year-old missing for three
                days now—new snow and meltoff

on this bright morning have left little
                to guess with and we trudge east in
      teams of four, taking turns calling her
                name so three can save what little

heat remains under layers of flannel
                and wool. Warm air exhaled dampens,
      ices over the outside of scarves and
                ski masks, and we look like we

breathe ice, are living cold born of
                this January morning. Dogs ahead
      have stopped and bark as if they have
                treed another squirrel, but when

we reach them circling what might be
        a snow-covered rock beside a creek,
    we each know it isn't, know this morning
            is colder than any morning we'll ever

know, and when one of us leans over her,
        brushes the snow from her back and it
    glitters as the wind catches and holds it up
            in the sun, we all look away from one

another. Then one of us goes to lead others
        here and we clear the snow from her,
    try to turn her to her back, but the hands
            have frozen to the ice of the bank—

lifting tears the skin from the palm—
        so we stop. One man pulls a blanket
    from his pack, kneels beside her and
            tenderly covers her from boots to out-

stretched fingers. The dogs have found
        a break in the ice farther up the creek
    where water manages to trickle through
            and they crowd about to drink. We

have wandered apart: one watching behind
        for the other searchers, another pulling
    off his gloves to light a cigarette,
            the last whistling sharply for the dogs.

ISINGLASS

Every La Quinta and Holiday Inn booked
their last room and each square inch
of closet space and final cubic millimeter

of air to the horde of Shriners and football fans
who planned their simultaneous invasion
months ago. Little Rock hasn't seen action

like this since Central High, or at least
the Election Night assault that left the town
dizzy in tattered red, white, and blue

for a favorite son whose lustre dimmed
too quickly. Friday night the sons
of Abou Ben Adhem unfurled their standards

on every dance floor—"Super Freak,"
"Blue Suede Shoes," "Orange Blossom Special"—
they hustled and twisted and cotton-eye-joed,

spinning in crazier circles than their midget cars
and four-wheelers twisted in afternoon
parading from the Capitol to Convention Center.

From Tennessee and Texas, Oklahoma,
Missouri, Louisiana and here, they've spilled
out of all the backroad towns and cities

secreted across the middle south,
a nowhere somewhere region the compass
never settles on, and now they've found

their direction, on target for every pitcher-
beer dive, honkytonk strip club, all-night
hotel watering hole where they shake

the walls like the big one's finally here—
and it is, upstairs where a drunken
Dallas Shriner bellows, *Get me the Manager!*

like only a Texan who spends his mornings
roping scrawny heifers on a ranch he keeps up
just for show can. The night clerk has

the thousand-yard stare of a soldier
who has seen too much, and she surrenders,
reluctantly handing over the last key.

Morning belongs to the football fans
in their red plastic hog hats, pig snouts,
transforming themselves into swine

for tailgate parties in front of War Memorial
Stadium. Echoes of *Woo Pig Sooie*
rebound across the parking lot in sporadic

displays of enthusiasm for a team they hope
will play .500 ball; still it's not the game
or winning or losing that brings them here,

but the communal grunting and hollering
rising from bellies and bowels to unsettle
the first signs of fall chill, glint of color

in the surrendering leaves, scrim of spectacle
glimmering as sun flashes off bright trumpets
and trombones, tubas and majorettes

trapped down on the field's glare
like they're plastered back behind a slick
thin sheet of mica clamping tight

and distorting each framed moment
squirming for life underneath the shiny
pane in someone's keepsake album.

For all the noise and hoopla trying
to beat its way into the brain, the real
auto-da-fé, carnival and freakshow,

your show of shows, crawls its way
along here, back at the Hilton,
where hopeful parents hustle newborns

and toddlers dolled up with rouge
and mascara—just a touch of berry-red
lipstick for that five-thousand-dollar

pout. These baby-show dreamers
picture little Emmanuel and Tiffany,
Shadrey and Adam as the next Coppertone

Ivory Snow Jack-in-the-Box
American advertising whiz kids
selling home, mother, and Chevrolet

with a smile or a tear, so they've packaged,
primped, primed, and delivered the goods
with 8 x 10 glossies, Sunday best spit

and polish. But behind bright eyes,
these little show ponies stumble
and right themselves with a frightened

tremor, a quiver bit under bee-stung
lips and pinched cheeks, the first sign
of the quake that shakes tight curls

and plastered bangs, the ribbons
and bow-ties which are so perfectly,
terminally, meticulously out of place.

My Brother, Betting on Ray's Hope

The track favors mudders, but you pick her anyway—
she shares your middle name and the form shows
she's run a fast mile and a quarter at Louisiana Downs.
I point out it was a dry track in Shreveport, but somehow
I know she'll come in as long as I don't put any money
on her. The horses don't like me, but you've got luck—
your life a sure thing, like a fast horse with a good
jockey. I'm moving to Corpus Christi for a job
I can't wait to get out of, but no one's saying, *Don't go,*
not even you—the money's good, I'm out of school,
it's a warm climate, even with hurricane season.
The rain stops before the race and we're able to find
a place at the rail as the thoroughbreds saunter toward
the gates. An old man walks by, his Cardinals cap
on backwards. He sells peanuts and cigarettes, but
for two bucks he'll do a cartwheel and somersault,
for three, an Ozzie Smith running forward flip.
A man with a gold money clip starts bargaining him
down, but then—*They're off!*—and the announcer's call
drowns out everything but the woman screaming,
Go Rabbithead! They come into the stretch and we
all lean forward. I'm surprised the rail holds, but
it does, and you wave your winning ticket like the air
sanctifies it. The woman has stopped screaming,
tears her tickets in half. You buy dinner, and before
the drive back to Little Rock, we stop at Hot Springs
National Park. It's only a grotto filled with algae
and a couple of water fountains, but I press the button

on the sign and we listen to the story of de Soto
and the spring. When it's finished, I dip my hand
in the pool and you toss a quarter in. At the fountains
we drink like we believe the minerals will be good
for us, like we'll take something that will last.
On the drive, you shuffle through tip sheets and forms
we should have thrown away at the track and ask
if I've thought of crossing the border for races there,
maybe even bullfights. I laugh, tell you no, I've
decided I'm not good at gambling. The glass keeps
fogging up and you search the floorboard for a towel,
wipe the windshield until you know I see the road.

Blue Crabs

As we walk by the sandstone gate,
I admit you were right about this trip—
It seems we've gone too far again.

Goose Island long out of season,
its shore and pier empty except
for snowbirds from Wisconsin

and two teenagers working
surf rigs. The boys' beat-up
VW sits right on the water,

its splotchy shell some great
sea turtle depositing its eggs
in the hard sand. No danger

of tide here and the boys don't
stand a chance in this stagnant
lagoon, but they continue casting

into the black-green algae
clotting the water, cursing
when their sharp red and silver

torpedoes snag and drag back
a blooming mass. The couple
from Wisconsin has a better idea.

Lounging halfway down the pier
in their straw hats, they raise
and lower crab traps they've

tied to the aluminum chairs.
The old man cuts perch for
bait while his wife rotates

traps in and out of the water,
depositing the catch in a green
ice chest situated between them.

When we reach their spot, exchange
pleasantries, the man lifts back
the cooler's lid and offers us four

from the squirming tangle
of brown-white-turquoise claws.
He says they have far too many

despite his wife's glares; but
we have nothing to hold them
so we thank him and decline.

The pier stretches out toward
the lip of this shallow bay
and we follow it past herons

and egrets flanking the wooden
pilings with stoic reflections,
gulls shimmering down and back

in the bright wind. A fisherman
left a ray drying on the planks
and we must step carefully over

its bedeviled leather. Crab shells
litter spots we pass, green bottle
flies swarming around the eyes,

jaundiced organs and deadman left
behind. You speak of hard-shells
your father would boil back in

the Bronx, steam whistling from
them like a warning. We find
ourselves far from home on this

brackish South Texas shoreline,
no sense to the migrations that
have brought us here, jobs no

better than the traps the blue crabs
scuttle into—some scraps of food,
an illusion of security. Our single

consolation comes from being
together—more than your parents
had when they left warm islands

for the chill of England. The rocky
land in Jamaica, cattle and goats
on the hillsides of Carriacou

offered little promise for a future,
far too late now to second-guess
if Britain, Canada, America made

better choices. My parents crossed
state lines, not oceans; leaving
the red clay of Alabama for Iowa,

Nebraska, Arkansas. Our journeys
might go short or long; it doesn't
matter. Beyond us, in the open

water, two pilot whales breach and
blow spouts of sparkling mist into
the sunlight. Their dark backs

break the waves before diving, and
we know as we imagine maps
and routes they wander, wherever

they head toward is home. As
we stand against this constant
wind, we still know the way.

ENOUGH

Rain slick tracks of tires
disappearing as we pull away,
five A.M. bundles of tragedy

dotting the corners like news
of a past day. Flash by
serious travelers wasting

no light, no time to hurry
someplace else, each and every
destination departing—

gate three, no standby,
foreign and domestic locations
within reach—beyond curling

smoke bending from ashtrays,
dissipating like imagination,
exotic ports of call no more

than Greensboro, Mishawaka,
Newark. When the plane loads,
lumbers off across tarmac

and whistles its way up
into the first burnt clouds
streaking violet above pine

and river in the distance,
I'll watch you disappear like
a last sweet taste of licorice.

Testimony Bed

I know the faces of hate that curl
around our passing like shell casings
hickory nuts shed each autumn twist
back into a hard knot of useless wrapping.

Wrecked-car, tar-paper neighborhood
where every other fence held back
a "white dog" nurtured on fury waiting
to unleash on any passing dark face.

Side by side we cannot pass out of sight
in enough of a hurry without these
small Southern towns turning sinister
as our past and present history—

classmates beside me in first grade asked
to pass along notes "encouraging"
their parents to consider "majority-minority
schools" less than a decade after Central High.

The Midwest was a heavy white blanket
we smothered beneath as an invisible novelty,
but in Little Rock the battle lines are as clear
as the faces of the children we pass by,

their small hands clinging to the dark or light
hand of the parent on watch, a mother
or father whose glance passing our direction
carries more knowing than either of us has.

It is not political nor politic, not temporary
nor ever likely to simply pass without some
notice, but when we intertwine our fingers
and walk together we give witness to lives

and a nation where so much depends upon
who you pass each night beside, what truth
lingers each morning in promises that dress
the bed tighter than any white sheet ever could.

ACKNOWLEDGMENTS

Acknowledgment is made to the following publications for poems that originally appeared in them or are forthcoming.

Black Zinnias – "Slow Light"

Brilliant Corners – "Pers'nal Use"

Calliope – "Lunar Eclipse," "Enough," and "Play Pretties"

Concelebratory Shoehorn Review – "Dogwood Creek," "Magnolia," and "Testimony Bed"

Contemporary American Voices – "Every Day," "The Garden," and "Whisper Trees"

Crazyhorse – "First Rites: Devil's Den State Park," "Imago Mundi," and "We Are Part of the Body"

Dublin Poetry Review – "Amateur Night at the Prime Tyme"

Ghost Town – "Driver's School" and "Hookslide"

The Jazz Poetry Anthology – "Anaximander Lewis"

North Dakota Quarterly – "Labor Day"

Ploughshares – "My Brother, Betting on Ray's Hope"

Poetry – "Fathers"

A Poetry Congeries from Connotation Press – "Conversations with the Dead"

Prime Number – "Blue Crabs"

Riverrun – "From the West" and "Tunnel"

Rosebud – "Nightwatchman"

Southeast Review – "Isinglass" and "White Boy with Afro"

storySouth – "The Day After Elvis Died" and "Up and Down Wye Mountain"

Surreal South – "The Best Chicken in Arkansas" and "Cactus Vic and His Marvelous Magical Elephant"

The entirety or lines from "Up and Down Wye Mountain" and "Whisper Trees" were reprinted in *Pirene's Fountain: A Journal of Poetry* (Volume 7, Issue 15).

I want to thank all my teachers, colleagues, and friends who have helped me realize the possibilities of these poems over the years, especially Ralph Burns, David Jauss, Rodney Jones, Yusef Komunyakaa, Roger Mitchell, Maura Stanton, and David Wojahn. Special thanks to Carolyn Alessio, Stacey Lynn Brown, Adrian Matejka, and, of course, Allison Joseph, who insisted throughout the years I was a poet as well as an editor. And thank you to Ami Kaye and everyone at Glass Lyre Press.

ABOUT THE AUTHOR

Jon Tribble was born in Little Rock, Arkansas. He grew up in Aldersgate Camp, a church camp devoted to medical and social services programming just outside of Little Rock. He has worked as a dishwasher, maintenance worker, fry cook, movie theater manager, data processing clerk, and nightwatchman, and he has lived in Arkansas, South Texas, Indiana, and Illinois. He was the recipient of the 2001 Campbell Corner Poetry Prize and he received a 2003 Illinois Arts Council Fellowship in Poetry. He has published poems in print journals, including *Ploughshares, Poetry, Crazyhorse, Brilliant Corners,* and the *Southeast Review*; online, including in *Prime Number, A Poetry Congeries at Connotation Press: An Online Artifact,* and *storySouth*; and in several anthologies, including *The Jazz Poetry Anthology* and *Where We Live: Illinois Poets.* He lives in Carbondale, Illinois, with his wife, Allison Joseph, and he directs internships in editing and publishing for the Department of English at Southern Illinois University Carbondale. He is the Managing Editor of the literary journal *Crab Orchard Review* and is the Series Editor of the Crab Orchard Series in Poetry from SIU Press.

Glass Lyre Press

exceptional works to replenish the spirit

Glass Lyre Press is an independent literary publisher interested in technically accomplished, stylistically distinct, and original work. Glass Lyre seeks diverse writers that possess a dynamic aesthetic and an ability to emotionally and intellectually engage a wide audience of readers.

Glass Lyre's vision is to connect the world through language and art. We hope to expand the scope of poetry and short fiction for the general reader through exceptionally well-written books, which evoke emotion, provide insight, and resonate with the human spirit.

Poetry Collections
Poetry Chapbooks
Select Short & Flash Fiction
Anthologies

www.GlassLyrePress.com

CPSIA information can be obtained at www.ICGtesting.com
Printed in the USA
LVOW12s2313170216

475565LV00002B/3/P

9 781941 783153